Over the Moon

COMPLETE PRIMARY ENGLISH LANGUAGE PROGRAMME

Going on Holidays

Mary O'Keeffe

GILL EDUCATION

We live here.

We like it here, but we like to go on **holidays** too.

Holidays are lots of fun.

Meg and Mel like to play.

Mam and Dad like to sit in the sun.

The dog can't come, as we have to go on a jet.

She is a bit sad.

"The dog can go to Nan's," said Mam.

Nan and the dog will go on lots of trips.

The dog likes Nan.

She gives Nan a lick.

She will miss us, but she will have fun with Nan.

It is Dad's job to get the **suitcase**.

Mam will lend him a hand.

There is a lot to do.

Mam helps Meg and Mel to pack for the **holidays**.

One by one, I put my bits and bobs into my **suitcase**.

I put my big van in.

It was fun to pack my
suitcase!

Come on! Let's go!

"Have you got your ted?" said Dad.

Oh no! Quick!

I do not want to be the last to get into the car.

I will have to sit by Meg and Mel.

I do not want to sit by Meg and Mel!

They like to have fun and mess.

They like to be daft.

I do not like to be daft.

I like to rest for my **holidays**.

Oh no!

Oh well.

I will just have to be daft like Meg and Mel.

Let's go on **holidays**!